Constitution

The Russian Federation

With Commentaries and Interpretation
by American and Russian Scholars

DISCARD

Edited by
Vladimir V. Belyakov
and
Walter J. Raymond

Brunswick and Novosti

Library of Congress Cataloging-in-Publication Data

Russia (Federation)
    [Konstitutsiia (1993). English]
    Constitution of the Russian Federation : with commentaries
and interpretations / by American and Russian scholars ; edited
by Vladimir V. Belyakov and Walter J. Raymond. -- 1st ed.
        p.   cm.
    ISBN 1-55618-143-4 (acid-free paper) : $35.00. --
    ISBN 1-55618-142-6 (pbk. : alk. paper) : $12.00
    1. Russia (Federation)--Constitution. 2. Russia (Federation) --
Constitutional law.   I. Belyakov, Vladimir, V., 1936-
II. Raymond, Walter John, 1930-   III. Title.
KLB2064.51993.B45   1994
342.47'023--dc20
[344.70223]   94-4723
                                                           CIP

First Edition
Published in the United States of America
by

Brunswick Publishing Corporation
Rt. 1, Box 1A1
Lawrenceville, Virginia 23868
and
Russia's Information Agency-Novosti
Moscow, the Russian Federation

To the great Russian People and their leader,
President Boris Nikolayevich Yeltsin

THE EDITORS

Vladimir V. Belyakov, educated at Moscow universities, serves currently as a Counselor and Head of the Information Department of the Embassy of the Russian Federation in Washington, D.C., and Editor-in-Chief of Russia's Information Agency-Novosti with offices in Moscow and Washington, D.C., and their publication in the United States, *Russian Life*.

Walter J. Raymond, a Ph.D. in Political Science and S.J.D. in Law and Jurisprudence, is an educator, publisher and author of *Dictionary of Politics: Selected American and Foreign Political and Legal Terms,* 7th ed., and other studies in government and politics.

CONTENTS

Introduction 1

The New Russian Constitution: Social Validity
    by *Alexander M. Yakovlev* 3

A Brief Comparative Analysis of the Russian Constitution
    by *Ronald C. Monticone* 7

APPENDIXES

A. Constitution of the Russian Federation 15

B. Blocs, Factions, Parties: The Political Anatomy of
    the new Parliament of the Russian Federation—
    the State Duma 78

C. Speakers of the State Duma and the
    Federation Council 79

D. The Government of the Russian Federation.................... 80

E. Leaders of the Soviet Union and the Russian
    Federation Since the Abdication of the
    Last Monarch... 81

F. The Former Soviet Union (USSR) 83

MAPS

The Former Soviet Union and the Russian Federation 84

The Russian Federation and Ethnic Russians in the
    Former Soviet Union... 86

INTRODUCTION

The new Russian Constitution is a product of the Russian mind, influenced in some ways by constitutional models elsewhere. And in spite of its possible shortcomings, it is the best document that Russia can present at this time. Therefore, all of us outside Russia should offer constructive help so that this experiment can continue. The Russian Constitution, just like any other modern constitution, will, no doubt, be subjected to revisions and modifications in response to internal and external developments.

The Constitution is also the product of minds of a political entity which just yesterday was an empire and which transformed itself, without a major internal conflict, into a multinational federation. Being no doubt cognizant of the fact that most states today do not adhere to the provisions of their constitutions, the writers put together a document which, in their opinion, can and must be adhered to, in order to avoid chaos and political calamity. The document reveals understanding on the part of its writers of the internal and external political landscapes following the post-imperial era. The Constitution, the basic law of a large, multinational state in modern times, does what is politically possible and what is realistic; it is a product of an experimentation in the governance of a complex society amid very rapid changes. Therefore, any society, and particularly a major global power, which is undergoing rapid changes in order to feed and house its people, maintain internal peace and tranquility, and, at the same time, contribute to global peace and security, should be viewed by all with admiration and willingness to help, with an open mind and an open heart!

The current constitutional experiment in the Russian Federation is a noble beginning!

THE PUBLISHERS

THE NEW RUSSIAN CONSTITUTION: SOCIAL VALIDITY

By Alexander M. Yakovlev

An estimation of any legal acts, constitutions included, presupposes an implication of at least two levels of analysis. First, an interpretation of the text of the constitution at its face value, and second, an attempt to estimate its place in the social and historical realities of a given country. I will limit this commentary on the 1993 Constitution of the Russian Federation to the problems of economic and political rights as they have direct relevance to the central constitutional problem: the social validity—the real significance—of this Constitution as a whole.

These rights and liberties can be subdivided into two groups: the political (or so-called "negative") rights and the economic and social (so-called "positive") rights. Negative rights: freedom of expression, inviolability of the person and of the dwelling place, freedom of association, freedom of conscience, freedom of movement, etc. Positive rights: the right to work, the right to a paid holiday, the right to recreation, the right to guaranteed free medical service, the right to an adequate living standard, the right to education, etc. Both kinds of rights are present in the 1993 Constitution of the Russian Federation. An estimation of the

---

Dr. Alexander Maximovich Yakovlev is the Plenipotentiary of the President of the Russian Federation in the Federal Assembly, a Professor and Doctor of Law, a world renown Russian jurist, and a section head at the State and Law Institute of Russia's Academy of Sciences in Moscow.

social and political significance of inclusion in the Constitution of the Russian Federation of these rights reveals one of the crucial problems of constitutional development in Russia.

In his article "Against Positive Rights" Cass Sustein came to the conclusion that inclusion in Eastern European constitutions of this "chaotic catalogue of abstractions from the social welfare state . . . is a large mistake, possibly a disaster" (*East European Constitutional Review,* Vol. 1 No. 2 1992). He stresses the specificity of the problems confronting the countries in the period of transition from communism to a market economy, the most serious among them being the establishment of government interference with free markets as a constitutional obligation. Sustein argues that to ensure for citizens adequate living conditions is a problem not for the "state" but for "decent" society itself and the relevant provision can be provided in special programs but not in the constitution. Furthermore he points out that the most important problems for the countries in question is to undo "the culture of dependency," to diminish the sense of entitlement to state protection, and to encourage individual initiative.

The positive rights enumerated above are provided for in the 1993 Constitution of the Russian Federation (see Articles 37-3, 37-5, 39, 40, 41, 42, 43). In this connection some points could be added to this argumentation. In the former Soviet Union, the USSR Constitution was also providing for positive rights, among them free health care, free education, and free housing. To outsiders these free economic benefits may look like some kind of socialist utopia come true. But it is important to recognize several things: a) these "gifts" are fictitious, since they had been already paid for by the workers whose wage was severely restricted, dictated by the state; b) the extremely low, substandard level of the "ordinary" (not the privileged) kind of health services, housing, education facilities cannot realistically be improved without privatization. To the extent that there was equality, it was equality in poverty.

The price of these "benefits" was extremely high. The extermination of private property, delegalization of market relations and establishment of a system based on distribution of goods and services provided exclusively by the state resulted in economic enslavement of the people; any attempt to economic activities outside of the state monopoly were punished as a crime; this loss of freedom was accompanied by the creation of a huge, mammoth bureaucracy—the distributors of the very necessities of life, the real dispensers of life and death for the whole country. The existence of this structure made a mockery of the civil and political rights also provided for in the USSR Constitution. The political lesson that can be learned from the Russian experience is that the claim of a state to be "benefactor" for the people, to provide for the welfare of everyone, to substitute (for the sake of this aim) state property and planned economy for private property and market economy, results in misery and tyranny.

Now in Russia the political and economic transformation of tremendous proportions is in progress. Two forces are opposing each other: a relatively small but dynamic private sector and a much larger, but stagnating, state controlled one. The spread of market relations brings the differentiation in wealth, real necessity for people to create a culture of self-reliance, enterprise, rising the rate of production, taking risks, facing the possibility to prosper or get bankrupt, etc. Inevitably, the society became polarized. The younger you are, the more marketable your profession, the more competitive you will be, and the less you will be tempted to be seduced by the promises of "instant welfare" provided by the state though redistribution at the price of giving away your newly acquired freedom. The older you are, the fewer possibilities exist for you to successfully compete, and the more you became inclined to ask (to demand!) the government to provide you with everything (the Constitution promised that). The conclusion, confirmed time and again, that if you agreed to forgo your freedom for the sake of prosperity, you will end up having neither prosperity nor the freedom, will not be easy for them to remember.

The alluring political effect of the populist tactics was confirmed by the December 1993 elections to the Russian parliament, the Federal Assembly. In the socialist teachings the idea of production is constantly ousted by the idea of distribution. The real welfare is the final product of the developed market economy, based on high productivity and national wealth. The same idea used under the conditions of scarcity will curtail productivity, will make again unreal not only the new Russian Constitution but democratic development as a whole as well.

A BRIEF COMPARATIVE ANALYSIS
OF THE RUSSIAN CONSTITUTION

By Ronald C. Monticone

The Constitution of the Russian Federation created a true federation with a division of powers between the central government and the local governments. In this respect, it is unlike its predecessors, the Constitutions of 1924, 1936 and 1977.[1] These three constitutions created a federation in theory only, where the various nationalities were supposed to exercise cultural and political autonomy. However, each of the nationalities was represented by communists. In the federal as well as in the local legislatures, they voted only for programs approved by the Politburo of the Central Committee of the Communist Party of the Soviet Union which was composed of the top leaders of the Communist Party of the Soviet Union. In most federations, the local governments are permitted to levy taxes and dispose of revenues as they wish. In the former Soviet Union, the federal government denied the local governments the right to tax and dispose of income except in accordance with the terms established by federal authorities. The federal parliament adopted a budget

Dr. Ronald C. Monticone received a Ph.D. from New York University in the field of Comparative Government and is currently a Professor of Political Science at the Queensborough Campus of the City University of New York. He is the author of a political biography on *Charles de Gaulle* and a monograph on the *Catholic Church in Communist Poland, 1945-1985*. Dr. Monticone is a member of the Board of Editors of the *Polish Review,* a scholarly quarterly on Polish and East European Affairs. He has written several articles and book reviews for a number of scholarly journals.

7

for the entire nation. In most federations, the local governments have the right to vote on amendments to the constitution. In the former Soviet Union, the federal parliament had the sole right to approve amendments. It also had the right to annul laws passed by local parliaments and could also annul decrees of the executive branch of the local governments. Therefore, the Soviet Union was not truly a federation until Gorbachev's reforms were implemented between 1989-1991.

The Constitution of the United States allows its people to exercise power indirectly by voting for members of the federal and state legislative and executive branches. The new Russian Constitution not only allows its people to exercise power indirectly by voting for members of federal and local bodies of authority, but it allows them to exercise power directly, as in France, by voting in referenda.

The U.S. Constitution specifies that powers not delegated to the federal government nor denied to the states are reserved to the states and to the people. Therefore, subjects not mentioned in the Constitution of the U.S. are powers reserved to the states and to the people. The Constitution of the Russian Federation is similar to the Constitution of the United States in this respect. It delegates powers to the federal government and enumerates the powers which can be exercised concurrently by the federal government and the member units and then stipulates that the member units may exercise powers not mentioned in the constitution. The Constitution of the Federal Republic of Germany reserves even more powers to the local governments (state governments) of Germany than the U.S. and Russian Constitutions reserve to their local governments.

Unlike its three predecessors, the new Russian Constitution allows a mixed economy both capitalist and socialist like the countries of Western Europe and recognizes ideological pluralism. The Constitutions of 1924, 1936 and 1977 mandated a one party totalitarian socialist state at least until the Gorbachev amendments were added to the Constitution of 1977.

All basic civil rights, including separation of Church and State and freedom of religion, exist not only in theory as they did in the past but in practice as is true in western democracies. These rights may be exercised by all inhabitants regardless of sex, social, racial, national, language or religious affiliation. Under the three previous constitutions, civil rights could only be exercised in the interests of the people and the Communist Party of the Soviet Union, which defined the interests of the people, and determined if and when civil rights could be exercised.

Whereas the Constitution of the United States is vague and ambiguous and therefore broad enough to be interpreted in many different ways as expediency demands, the new Constitution of the Russian Federation is specific down to the most minute detail and even addresses matters like working conditions, the care of children, social security, state pensions and social benefits, housing, health protection and medical care, education, dual citizenship and asylum.

The Constitution of the Russian Federation, like the Constitution of the United States, indicates that the federal constitution is the supreme law and therefore laws that conflict with the federal constitution are null and void. The Constitutions of the United States and the Russian Federation both contain supremacy clauses which indicate that whenever there is a conflict between a federal law and a law of a local legislature, the federal law is supreme and therefore takes precedence.

Great Britain and the Federal Republic of Germany are prototypes of a parliamentary system of government where the prime minister and the cabinet (the executive branch, known as the government) must be members of parliament. In the United States, which is the prototype of a presidential system of government, the Constitution provides that no member of one branch of government may serve on either of the other two branches at the same time so as to ensure separation of powers. The Constitution of the Fifth Republic of France (current government of France) provides for a combination presidential-parliamentary system of government, where the prime minister and the cabinet (government) may not sit in parliament, yet the lower house of parliament may censure the government and cause it to resign. The new Constitution of the Russian Federation forbids any member of the lower house of parliament (State Duma) to serve in either the executive or the judicial branches of government while serving in the lower house of parliament. This same Constitution is silent as to whether a member of the upper house of the Russian parliament (Federal Council) may serve in either of the other two branches while serving in the upper house of parliament. The lower house of the Russian parliament may censure the government just as the lower house of the French parliament may censure the government. However, the lower house of the French parliament may not censure the President of France and the lower house of the Russian parliament may not censure the President of Russia, who, like the President of France and the President of the United States, has considerable power in both domestic and foreign affairs.[2]

The President of Russia is the head of state and guarantor of the Constitution of the Russian Federation and of human rights and freedoms. He is the protector of the sovereignty, independence and state integrity of the Russian Federation and determines the guidelines for domestic and foreign policy. With the consent of the lower house of parliament, the State Duma, he appoints the Chairman of the Government of the Russian Federation (prime minister), appoints members of the government after they have been proposed by the Chairman of the Government, nominates judges to the Constitutional Court, Supreme Court, Court of Arbitration of the Russian Federation, the Prosecutor-General of the Russian Federation and appoints judges to other federal courts. He appoints and dismisses top commanders of the Armed Forces of the Russian Federation and appoints and recalls diplomatic representatives to foreign countries. He conducts the foreign policy of and is commander-in-chief of the armed forces of the Russian Federation. He has the power to call elections to the State Duma, dissolve the State Duma in accordance with the circumstances stipulated in the Constitution, call a referendum, submit bills to the State Duma and sign federal laws. He decides questions of Russian citizenship, and may grant political asylum and pardons. From these powers one can see that the President of the Russian Federation exercises control over almost every policy.

The relationship between the President and the Prime Minister of the Russian Federation under the new Constitution is similar to the relationship between the President and the Prime Minister of France in the

Fifth Republic. However, the relationship between the cabinet including the prime minister and the parliament of the new Russian Federation resembles the British system in some respects and the French system in others. As in France, the prime minister and the cabinet may not sit in the lower house of parliament of the Russian Federation, but the lower house of parliament may censure the government. Unlike France, however, in case the government is censured and receives a vote of no confidence in the lower house of parliament, the President of the Russian Federation determines whether to dismiss the government or dissolve the lower house of parliament and call for new elections. Although this same choice exists in Great Britain, it is the prime minister who makes this choice. In France, the president must name a new prime minister who will then appoint a new cabinet if the lower house of parliament censures the government. From this fact it would seem as if parliament in France is powerful compared to its counterpart in Great Britain, but in reality the French parliament is the weakest legislature of any western democracy, and not once has the French parliament censured the government during the entire period of the Fifth Republic (1959-present). The legislature of the new Russian Federation is weak compared to the president just as the legislature of France is weak compared to its president. So are the legislatures of Great Britain and the Federal Republic of Germany weak compared to their prime ministers.

The federal court system of Russia resembles that of other western democracies. The right of judicial review, that is to say the right of courts to review the constitutionality of laws if asked to do so, is a very interesting subject. In the United States, courts, including the Supreme Court, may review the constitutionality of laws provided that these laws are challenged by an individual or a group. The Supreme Court is the highest appellate court of the United States and only has original jurisdiction over cases involving ambassadors, ministers of foreign countries, consuls of foreign countries or if one of the fifty states is a direct party to the dispute. Therefore, most constitutional issues that come before the Supreme Court are heard on appeal. In the Federal Republic of Germany, the Federal Constitutional Court is a court of original jurisdiction. Individuals in Germany may take their case to the Federal Constitutional Court when they feel that their civil rights have been violated, but departments and agencies of the federal and state governments may call on the Federal Constitutional Court to interpret the Constitution. Disputes between the federal and state governments may also be settled by the Federal Constitutional Court. In Britain there is no tradition of judicial review since there is no written constitution. In France, the Constitutional Council must review the constitutionality of every law passed by the French parliament before it can go into effect. In the new Russian Federation, the Constitutional Court will review laws if requested to do so by the President of the Russian Federation, the Supreme Court of the Russian Federation, the Supreme Arbitration Court of the Russian Federation and local legislative and executive bodies. Article 125, paragraph 4, allows individuals to take their cases to the Constitutional Court in original jurisdiction if they feel that their constitutional rights and freedoms have been violated. So it seems as if the Constitutional Court in the Russian Federation performs a role more similar to that of the Federal Constitutional Court of Germany than to the Supreme Court of the United States or the Constitutional Council of France.

The Constitution of the Russian Federation creates a genuine western democracy. There is, however, an old adage that a constitution will succeed only if it reflects the wishes of the people for whom it is written. It will not succeed if it reflects only the wishes of the people who wrote it. We genuinely hope that the new Constitution of the Russian Federation reflects the wishes of the people who inhabit that federation, and we wish them well.

NOTES

[1.] It is generally recognized throughout the world that the new Russian Federation is the successor not only of the old Russian Federation but of the Soviet Union as well. The new Russian Federation now occupies the seat on the Security Council of the United Nations formerly occupied by the Soviet Union, and in the past political scientists often referred to the Soviet Union as Russia. Therefore, the author compares the old Soviet Constitutions to the new Constitution of the Russian Federation.

[2.] Censorship refers to a vote of no confidence by a legislature in a government policy. It means that the legislature does not agree with the executive branch on a policy issue. Impeachment and removal is a different matter altogether. The legislatures of France, Russia and the United States may impeach and remove their presidents but only for grave offenses such as treason, bribery and other felonies and for misdemeanors like abuse of power, drunkenness and failure to perform duties.

Constitution of
The Russian Federation*

We, the multi-ethnic people of the Russian Federation,
United by our common destiny of our land,

Seeking to advance human rights and freedoms and promote civil peace and accord,

Preserving a historically established state unity,

Guided by universally recognized principles of equality and self-determination of peoples,

Honoring the memory of our ancestors, who bequeathed to us their love and respect for our homeland and their faith in goodness and justice,

Renewing the sovereign statehood of Russia and acknowledging the immutability of its democratic foundations,

Seeking to ensure Russia's well-being and prosperity,

Realizing our responsibility for our homeland for present and future generations,

Considering ourselves a part of the world community,

Adopt this CONSTITUTION OF THE RUSSIAN FEDERATION.

---

*The national referendum on the draft of the Constitution of the Russian Federation was held simultaneously with the elections to the Federal Assembly, the State Duma, on 12 December 1993. The draft was presented to the voters by the President of the Russian Federation, and 58,187,755 registered voters, or 54.08 percent, cast their ballots during the referendum. The final tally showed that as many as 32,937,630 voters, or 58.4 percent voted for the constitution, and 23,431,333, or 41.6 percent voted against it. Upon the final count of the votes, the Constitution was adopted and thus became the supreme law of the Federation.

PART ONE

Chapter 1.
The Principles of the Constitutional System

Article 1

1. The Russian Federation – Russia shall be a democratic, federative, law-based state with a republican form of government.

2. The names Russian Federation and Russia shall have one and the same meaning.

Article 2

Human beings and human rights and freedoms shall be of the highest value. Recognition of, respect for, and protection of the human and civil rights and freedoms shall be the duty of the state.

Article 3

1. The multi-ethnic people of the Russian Federation shall be the bearers of its sovereignty and the sole source of authority in the Russian Federation.

2. The people shall exercise their power directly and also through bodies of state authority and bodies of local self-government.

3. Referendums and free elections shall be the highest expression of the people's authority.

4. No person shall have the right to appropriate power in the Russian Federation. Seizure of power or appropriation of authority shall be prosecuted in accordance with federal law.

Article 4

1. The sovereignty of the Russian Federation shall extend to its entire territory.

2. The Constitution of the Russian Federation and federal laws shall have priority throughout the territory of the Russian Federation.

3. The Russian Federation shall ensure the integrity and inviolability of its territory.

Article 5

1. The Russian Federation shall be made up of republics, territories, regions, cities with federal status, the autonomous region and autonomous areas, all of which are equal members of the Russian Federation.

2. The republics (states) shall have their own constitutions and laws. Territories, regions, cities with federal status, the autonomous region and autonomous areas shall have their own statutes and laws.

3. The federative make-up of the Russian Federation shall be based upon its state integrity, a uniform system of state authority, the separation of jurisdiction and powers between the bodies of state authority of the Russian Federation and bodies of state authority of the members of the Russian Federation, and the equality and self-determination of the peoples within the Russian Federation.

4. All members of the Russian Federation shall be equal in their relations with federal bodies of state authority.

Article 6

1. Citizenship in the Russian Federation shall be acquired and revoked in accordance with federal law and

shall be uniform and equal regardless of how it was obtained

2. Each citizen of the Russian Federation shall have, throughout its territory, all rights and freedoms and shall carry equal duties as provided for in the Constitution of the Russian Federation.

3. No citizen of the Russian Federation shall be deprived of citizenship or of the right to change it.

Article 7

1. The Russian Federation shall be a social state, the policies of which shall aim to create conditions ensuring adequate living standards and the free development of every individual.

2. Citizens of the Russian Federation shall be guaranteed the protection of: their work and health, a minimum wage; state support for the family, motherhood, fatherhood, childhood, invalids, and aged people; the development of a system of social services; and the provision of state pensions, allowances and other social security guarantees.

. Article 8

1. A unified economic space, the free movement of commodities, services and finances, and support for competition and freedom of economic activity shall be guaranteed in the Russian Federation.

2. Private, state, municipal and other forms of property shall be equally recognized and protected in the Russian Federation

Article 9

1. Land and other natural resources shall be used and protected in the Russian Federation as the founda-

tion of life and the activity of the peoples living in the corresponding territory.

2. Land and other natural resources may become private, state, municipal and other forms of property.

Article 10

State power in the Russian Federation shall be exercised on the basis of its separation into legislative, executive and judicial branches. The bodies of legislative, executive and judicial power shall be independent from one another.

Article 11

1. State power in the Russian Federation shall be exercised by the President of the Russian Federation, the Federal Assembly (Federation Council and State Duma), the Government of the Russian Federation and the courts of law of the Russian Federation.

2. State power in the members of the Russian Federation shall be exercised by the bodies of state authority established by them.

3. The jurisdiction and powers between the bodies of state authority of the Russian Federation and the bodies of state authority of the members of the Russian Federation shall be delineated by this Constitution, the Federation Treaty and other treaties on the delineation of jurisdiction and powers.

Article 12

Local self-government shall be recognized and guaranteed in the Russian Federation. Local self-government shall be independent within the limits of its powers. The bodies of local self-government shall not be part of the system of the bodies of state authority.

Article 13

1. Ideological pluralism shall be recognized in the Russian Federation.

2. No ideology shall be established as a state or compulsory ideology.

3. Political diversity and a multi-party system shall be recognized in the Russian Federation.

4. All public associations shall be equal before the law.

5. The creation and activity of public associations whose purposes or actions are directed at forcibly changing the foundations of the constitutional system, disrupting the integrity of the Russian Federation, subverting the security of the state, creating armed units, or inciting social, racial, ethnic or religious strife, shall be prohibited.

Article 14

1. The Russian Federation shall be a secular state. No religion shall be declared an official or compulsory religion.

2. All religious associations shall be separate from the state and shall be equal before the law.

Article 15

1. The Constitution of the Russian Federation shall be the supreme law and shall be in force throughout the territory of the Russian Federation. No laws or other legislative acts passed in the Russian Federation shall contravene the Constitution of the Russian Federation.

2. Bodies of state authority and bodies of local self-

government, officials, citizens and their associations shall abide by the Constitution of the Russian Federation.

3. All laws shall be made public on an official basis. No law shall be passed if it has not been made public. No regulatory legal acts affecting human or civil rights, freedoms and duties shall be effective if they have not been made public officially.

4. Universally acknowledged principles and standards of international law and international treaties of the Russian Federation shall be a part of its legal system. Should an international treaty of the Russian Federation establish rules other than those established by law, the rules of the international treaty shall be applied.

Article 16

1. The provisions of this Chapter of the Constitution shall constitute the fundamental principles of the constitutional system of the Russian Federation and shall not be changed except in accordance with the procedure established by this Constitution.

2. No other provisions of this Constitution shall contradict the fundamental principles of the constitutional system of the Russian Federation.

Chapter 2. Human and Civil Rights and Freedoms

Article 17

1. Within the Russian Federation human and civil rights and freedoms shall be recognized and guaranteed under universally acknowledged principles and rules of

international law and in accordance with this Constitution.

2. Basic human rights and freedoms are inalienable and belong to each person from birth.

3. The exercise of human and civil rights and freedoms may not infringe on the rights and freedoms of other persons.

Article 18

Human and civil rights and freedoms shall be instituted directly. They shall determine the purpose, content and application of the laws, the work of legislative and executive authority and local self-government and shall be guaranteed by the justice system.

Article 19

1. All people shall be equal before the law and the court.

2. The state shall guarantee equal human and civil rights and freedoms without regard to sex, race, nationality language, origin, property or official status, place of residence, attitude toward religion, persuasions, affiliation with social associations or other circumstances. Any form of restriction of civil rights on the basis of social, racial, national, language or religious affiliation shall be prohibited.

3. Men and women shall have equal rights and freedoms and equal opportunities to exercise them.

Article 20

1. Each person shall have the right to life.

2. The death penalty, until its abolition, may be prescribed by federal law as an exceptional penalty for particularly grave crimes against life with the granting

to the accused of the right to have the case heard by a court with the participation of jurors.

Article 21

1. The dignity of the individual shall be protected by the state. Nothing may serve as a justification for its diminution.

2. No person shall be subjected to torture, violence or other cruel or degrading treatment or punishment. No person may be subjected to medical, scientific or other experiments without his/her voluntary consent.

Article 22

1. Each person shall have the right to freedom and personal inviolability.

2. Arrest, taking into custody and holding in custody shall only be authorized by a judicial decision. Without a judicial decision no person may be subjected to detention for a period of more than 48 hours.

Article 23

1. Each person shall have the right to the inviolability of private life, personal and family secrecy, and the protection of honor and good reputation.

2. Each person shall have the right to privacy of correspondence, telephone conversations, postal, telegraph and other messages. The restriction of this right shall only be allowed on the basis of a judicial decision.

Article 24

1. The gathering, storage, use and dissemination of information concerning the private life of an individual without the individual's consent shall not be allowed.

2. The bodies of state authority, the bodies of local self-government and their officials shall be obliged to provide each person access to documents and materials that directly affect his rights and freedoms unless otherwise specified in the law.

Article 25
The home shall be inviolable. No person shall have the right to enter a home against the will of the person(s) residing in it except in cases determined by federal law or on the basis of a judicial decision.

Article 26
1. Each person shall have the right to determine and indicate his nationality. No person may be forced to determine or indicate his nationality.

2. Each person shall have the right to use his native tongue and to choose freely the language of communication, upbringing, education, and artistic creation.

Article 27
1. Each person who is legitimately within the territory of the Russian Federation shall have the right to move freely and to choose where to live temporarily or permanently.

2. Each person may freely leave the boundaries of the Russian Federation. A citizen of the Russian Federation shall have the right to return to the Russian Federation without hindrance.

Article 28
Each person shall be guaranteed freedom of conscience and freedom of religion, including the right to profess individually or jointly with others any religion

or to profess none, to freely choose, hold and propagate religious and other beliefs and to act in accordance with them.

Article 29

1. Each person shall be guaranteed freedom of thought and speech.

2. No propaganda or agitation inciting social, racial, national or religious hatred and enmity shall be allowed. The propaganda of social, racial, national, religious or language supremacy shall be prohibited.

3. Nobody may be forced to express his opinions and persuasions or renounce them.

4. Each person shall have the right to freely seek, receive, transmit, produce and disseminate information in any legitimate way. The list of data that constitute state secrets shall be fixed by federal law.

5. Freedom of the mass media shall be guaranteed. Censorship shall he prohibited.

Article 30

1. Each person shall have the right to association, including the right to establish trade unions to safeguard his/her interests. Freedom of activity of public associations shall be guaranteed.

2. No person may be forced to join, or to maintain membership in, any association.

Article 31

Citizens of the Russian Federation shall have the right to assemble peacefully without arms, to hold meetings, rallies, demonstrations, processions, and to picket.

Article 32

1. Citizens of the Russian Federation shall have the right to participate in the management of state affairs both directly and through their representatives.

2. Citizens of the Russian Federation shall have the right to elect and be elected to bodies of state authority and bodies of local self-government and to participate in referendums.

3. Citizens found by a court not to be sui juris or held in places of detention under a court sentence shall not have the right to elect or be elected.

4. Citizens of the Russian Federation shall have equal access to state employment.

5. Citizens of the Russian Federation shall have the right to participate in the administration of justice.

Article 33

Citizens of the Russian Federation shall have the right to appeal personally and to send individual and collective appeals to state bodies and bodies of local self-government.

Article 34

1. Each person shall have the right to freely use his abilities and property for entrepreneurial or any other economic activity not prohibited by law.

2. No economic activities aimed at monopolization or unfair competition shall be allowed.

Article 35

1. The right of private ownership shall be protected by law.

2. Each person shall have the right to own property

and to possess, use and dispose of it both individually and jointly with other persons.

3. No person may be deprived of property except by a judicial decision. Compulsory alienation of property for state needs may only be carried out on the condition of prior and equal compensation.

4. The right of inheritance shall be guaranteed.

Article 36

1. Citizens and their associations shall be entitled to have land in private ownership.

2. The possession, use and disposal of land and other natural resources shall be exercised by the owners freely unless this inflicts damage on the environment and/or infringes the rights and legitimate interests of other persons.

3. The conditions or procedures for land use shall be determined on the basis of federal law.

Article 37

1. Labor shall be free. Each person shall have the right freely to dispose of his abilities to work and to choose a an occupation.

2. Compulsory labor shall be prohibited.

3. Each person shall have the right to work in conditions that meet the requirements of safety and hygiene, to remuneration for labor without any discrimination and not below the minimum wage established by federal law, as well as the right to protection against unemployment.

4. The right to individual and collective labor disputes with the employment of methods specified by federal law for their resolution, including the right to strike, shall be recognized.

5. Each person shall have the right to rest and leisure. A person working under a labor contract shall be guaranteed the length of working time, days off, holidays, and paid annual leave prescribed by federal law.

Article 38

1. Motherhood, childhood, and the family are under state protection.

2. The care of children and their upbringing shall be the equal right and duty of parents.

3. Able-bodied children who have reached the age of eighteen years shall take care of parents who are unable to work.

Article 39

1. Each person shall be guaranteed social security in old age, in the event of sickness, disability or loss of a family's primary provider, for the raising of children and in other cases specified by law.

2. State pensions and social benefits shall be established by law.

3. Voluntary social insurance, the creation of additional forms of social security and charity shall be encouraged.

Article 40

1. Each person shall have the right to housing. No person may be arbitrarily deprived of housing.

2. Bodies of state authority and bodies of local self-government shall encourage housing construction and create conditions for the exercise of the right to housing.

3. Housing shall be provided free or for a reasonable charge out of state, municipal and other housing

stocks to low-income and other persons indicated in the law who are in need of housing in accordance with procedures set by law.

Article 41

1. Each person shall have the right to health protection and medical assistance. Medical assistance in state and municipal health-care institutions shall be provided to citizens free of charge out of the resources of the appropriate budget, insurance premiums and other receipts.

2. Federal programs for the protection and improvement of the health of the population shall be financed. Measures to promote state, municipal and private systems of public health shall be taken. Activities conducive to improving the health of the individual, the development of physical culture and sports, and environmental, hygienic and epidemiological well-being shall be encouraged in the Russian Federation.

3. The withholding by officials of facts and circumstances that pose a threat to a person's life or health shall entail responsibility in accordance with federal law.

Article 42

Each person shall have the right to a favorable environment, reliable information on its condition and compensation for damage inflicted on his/her health or property by violations of environmental laws.

Article 43

1. Each person shall have the right to education.

2. Preschool, basic general and secondary vocational education in state or municipal educational insti-

tutions and at enterprises shall be guaranteed to be accessible to all citizens free of charge.

3. Each person shall be entitled on a competitive basis and free of charge to receive a higher education in a state or municipal educational institution or at an enterprise.

4. Basic general education shall be compulsory. Parents or guardians shall ensure that children obtain a basic general education.

5. The Russian Federation shall establish federal state educational standards and support various forms of education and self-education.

Article 44

1. Each person shall be guaranteed freedom of literary, artistic, scientific, technical and other types of creative work and teaching. Intellectual property shall be protected by law.

2. Each person shall have the right to participate in cultural life, to make use of cultural institutions, and to enjoy access to cultural activities and values.

3. Each person shall be obliged to care for the preservation of the historical and cultural heritage and cherish historical and cultural monuments.

Article 45

1. The state protection of human and civil rights and freedoms in the Russian Federation shall be guaranteed.

2. Each person shall be entitled to defend his/her rights and freedoms in every way not prohibited by law.

Article 46

1. Each person shall be guaranteed the judicial protection of his/her rights and freedoms.

2. Decisions and actions (or inaction) by bodies of state authority or bodies of local self-government, public associations or officials may be appealed in court.

3. Each person shall be entitled, in accordance with international treaties of the Russian Federation, to apply to inter-state bodies involved in the protection of human rights and freedoms if all available internal means of legal protection have been exhausted.

Article 47

1. No person may be deprived of the right to have a case examined in the court or by the judge to whose jurisdiction it is referred by law.

2. A person accused of committing a crime shall have the right to have a case heard by a court with the participation of jurors in the cases provided for by federal law.

Article 48

1. Each person shall be guaranteed the right to receive qualified legal assistance. In cases provided for by law legal assistance shall be provided free of charge.

2. Each person arrested, taken into custody or accused of committing a crime shall have the right to use the assistance of a lawyer (defense attorney) from the moment of arrest, being taken into custody, or the bringing of a charge, respectively.

Article 49

1. Each person accused of committing a crime shall be presumed innocent until his/her culpability is

proved in the manner specified by federal law and established by a court sentence which has become effective.

2. Defendants shall not be obliged to prove their innocence.

3. Irreconcilable doubts about the culpability of a person shall be interpreted in the defendant's favor.

Article 50

1. No person may be tried twice for the same crime.

2. Using evidence elicited in violation of federal law shall be inadmissible in administering justice.

3. Each person convicted of a crime shall have the right to a review of the sentence by a higher court in the manner specified by federal law, as well as the right to ask for a pardon or the lessening of a sentence.

Article 51

1. Citizens shall not be obliged to testify against themselves, their spouses or close relatives as specified by federal law.

2. Federal law may establish other cases in which citizens are relieved of the duty to give testimony.

Article 52

The rights of victims of crimes or abuses of authority shall be protected by law. The state shall provide victims access to justice and compensation for damage inflicted.

Article 53

Each person shall have the right to compensation by the state for damage inflicted by illegal actions (or inaction) of bodies of state authority or their officials.

Article 54

1. Laws establishing or heightening responsibility shall not have retroactive force.

2. No person may be held responsible for an act which at the time of its commission was not considered to be a violation of the law. If after the commission of a violation of the law the criminal responsibility for it has been abolished or mitigated, the new law shall apply.

Article 55

1. The enumeration in the Constitution of the Russian Federation of fundamental rights and freedoms shall not be interpreted as a denial or diminution of other generally recognized human and civil rights and freedoms.

2. Laws abolishing or diminishing human and civil rights and freedoms shall not be issued in the Russian Federation.

3. Human and civil rights and freedoms may be restricted by federal law only to the extent necessary for upholding the foundations of the constitutional system, morality, or the health, rights and lawful interests of other persons or for ensuring the defense of the country and state security.

Article 56

1. Individual restrictions on rights and freedoms, with an indication of the scope and time limits of their operation, may he imposed during a state of emergency to safeguard citizens' safety and uphold the constitutional system in accordance with federal constitutional law.

2. A state of emergency throughout the Russian

Federation and in its individual areas may be declared under circumstances and in the manner specified by federal constitutional law.

3. The rights and freedoms specified in Articles 20, 21, 23 (Part 1), 24, 28, 34 (Part 1), 40 (Part 1) and 46-54 of the Constitution of the Russian Federation shall not be subject to restriction.

Article 57

Each person shall be obliged to pay statutory taxes and levies. Laws imposing new taxes or worsening the position of the taxpayers shall not have retroactive force.

Article 58

Each person shall be obliged to protect nature and the environment and to treat natural wealth with care.

Article 59

1. Defense of the Fatherland shall be the duty and responsibility of citizens of the Russian Federation.

2. Citizens of the Russian Federation shall perform military service in accordance with federal law.

3. In cases where the performance of military service runs counter to a citizen's persuasions or religion, and also in other cases specified by federal law, a citizen of the Russian Federation shall have the right to replace military service with alternative civilian service.

Article 60

A citizen of the Russian Federation may independently exercise his/her rights and duties in full from the age of eighteen.

Article 61

1. A citizen of the Russian Federation may not be expelled from the Russian Federation or extradited to another state.

2. The Russian Federation shall guarantee its citizens defense and protection outside its boundaries.

Article 62

1. A citizen of the Russian Federation may have the citizenship of a foreign state (dual citizenship) in accordance with federal law or an international treaty of the Russian Federation.

2. A Russian Federation citizen's possession of the citizenship of a foreign state shall not detract from his/her rights or freedoms and shall not release him/her from the duties arising from Russian citizenship unless otherwise specified in federal law or an international treaty of the Russian Federation.

3. Foreign citizens and stateless persons in the Russian Federation shall enjoy rights and bear responsibilities on a par with the citizens of the Russian Federation, except in cases specified by federal law or an international treaty of the Russian Federation.

Article 63

1. The Russian Federation shall grant political asylum to foreign citizens and stateless persons in accordance with universally acknowledged rules of international law.

2. Extradition from the Russian Federation to other countries of persons being pursued for their political persuasions, or for actions (or inaction) that are not recognized as a crime in the Russian Federation, shall not be allowed. The extradition of persons accused of com-

mitting a crime, and the transfer of convicts for serving their punishment in other states, shall be carried out on the basis of federal law or an international treaty of the Russian Federation.

Article 64

The provisions of this Chapter shall be the basis of the legal status of the individual in the Russian Federation and may not be changed except in the manner specified in this Constitution.

Chapter 3. The Organization of the Federation

Article 65

1. The Russian Federation shall consist of the members of the Russian Federation:

the Republic of Adygeya (Adygeya), the Republic of Altai, the Republic of Bashkortostan, the Republic of Buryatia, the Republic of Daghestan, the Ingush Republic, the Kabardin-Balkar Republic, the Republic of Kalmykia – Khalmg Tangch, the Karachai-Circassian Republic, the Republic of Karelia, the Republic of Komi, the Republic of Marii El, the Republic of Mordovia, the Republic of Sakha (Yakutia), the Republic of North Ossetia, the Republic of Tatarstan (Tatarstan), the Republic of Tuva, the Udmurtian Republic, the Republic of Khakassia, the Chechen Republic, the Chuvash Republic – Chavash Republic;

The Altai Territory, the Krasnodar Territory, the Krasnoyarsk Territory, the Maritime Territory, the Stavropol Territory, the Khabarovsk Territory;

The Amur Region, the Arkhangelsk Region; the Astrakhan Region, the Belgorod Region, the Bryansk Region, the Vladimir Region, the Volgograd Region, the Vologda Region, the Voronezh Region, the Ivanovo Region, the Irkutsk Region, the Kaliningrad Region, the Kaluga Region, the Kamchatka Region, the Kemerovo Region, the Kirov Region, the Kostroma Region, the Kurgan Region, the Kursk Region, the Leningrad Region, the Lipetsk Region, the Magadan Region, the Moscow Region, the Murmansk Region; the Nizhny Novgorod Region, the Novgorod Region, the Novosibirsk Region, the Omsk Region, the Orenburg Region, the Oryol Region, the Penza Region, the Perm Region, the Pskov Region, the Rostov Region, the Ryazan Region, the Samara Region, the Saratov Region, the Sakhalin Region, the Sverdlovsk Region, the Smolensk Region, the Tambov Region, the Tver Region, the Tomsk Region, the Tula Region, the Tyumen Region, the Ulyanovsk Region, the Chelyabinsk Region, the Chita Region, the Yaroslavl Region;

Moscow, St. Petersburg – cities of federal importance;

The Jewish Autonomous Region;

The Aga Buryat Autonomous Area, the Komi-Permyak Autonomous Area, the Koryak Autonomous Area, the Nenets Autonomous Area, the Taimyr (Dolgan-Nenets) Autonomous Area, the Ust-Orda Buryat Autonomous Area, the Khanty-Mansi Autonomous Area, the Chukchi Autonomous Area, the Evenk Autonomous Area, the Yamal-Nenets Autonomous Area.

2. Admission into the Russian Federation or the establishment within it of a new member shall be per-

formed in the manner specified in a federal constitutional law.

Article 66

1. The status of a republic shall be defined by the Constitution of the Russian Federation and the constitution of the republic.

2. The status of a territory, region, city of federal importance, autonomous region or autonomous area shall be defined by the Constitution of the Russian Federation and the statutes of the territory, region, city of federal importance, autonomous region or autonomous area adopted by the legislative (representative) body of the relevant member of the Russian Federation.

3. Upon submission by the legislative and executive bodies of an autonomous region or autonomous area, a federal law on the autonomous region or autonomous area may be adopted.

4. The relations of autonomous areas that form part of a territory or region may be governed by federal law and a treaty between the bodies of state authority of the autonomous area and, respectively, the bodies of state authority of the territory or region.

5. The status of a member of the Russian Federation may be altered by the mutual consent of the Russian Federation and the member of the Russian Federation in accordance with a federal constitutional law.

Article 67

1. The territory of the Russian Federation shall comprise the territories of its members, inland waters and the territorial sea, and the airspace above them.

2. The Russian Federation shall have sovereign rights and exercise jurisdiction on the continental shelf

and in the exclusive economic zone of the Russian Federation in the manner specified by federal law and the rules of international law.

3. The boundaries between members of the Russian Federation may be changed with their mutual consent.

Article 68

1. The state language of the Russian Federation throughout its territory shall be the Russian language.

2. The republics shall have the right to establish their own state languages. In the bodies of state authority, bodies of local self-government and the state institutions of the republics they shall be used alongside the state language of the Russian Federation.

3. The Russian Federation shall guarantee all of its citizens the right to the preservation of their native tongue and the creation of conditions for its study and development.

Article 69

The Russian Federation shall guarantee the rights of indigenous ethnic minorities in accordance with universally acknowledged principles and rules of international law and the international treaties of the Russian Federation.

Article 70

1. The state flag, emblem and anthem of the Russian Federation, their description and manner of official use shall be established by a federal constitutional law.

2. The capital of the Russian Federation shall be the city of Moscow. The status of the capital shall be established by a federal law.

Article 71

The authority of the Russian Federation shall encompass:

a) the adoption and amendment of the Constitution of the Russian Federation and federal laws and supervision of their observance;

b) the organization of the federation and territory of the Russian Federation;

c) the regulation and protection of human and civil rights and freedoms; citizenship in the Russian Federation; the regulation and protection of the rights of national minorities;

d) the establishment of a system of federal bodies of legislative, executive and judicial authority, the manner of their organization and work; the setting up of federal bodies of state authority;

e) federal state property and the management thereof;

f) the establishment of principles of federal policy and federal programs in the area of state, economic, ecological, social, cultural and national development of the Russian Federation;

g) the establishment of legal principles for a single market; financial, foreign exchange, credit and customs control, issuance of money, the principles of pricing policy; federal economic services, including federal banks;

h) the federal budget; federal states and levies; federal funds for regional development;

i) federal energy systems, nuclear power engineering, fissionable materials; federal transport, railways, information and communications; space activity;

j) the foreign policy and international relations

of the Russian Federation, international treaties of the Russian Federation; issues of war and peace;

k) the external economic relations of the Russian Federation;

l) defense and security; defense production; the specification of the procedure for selling and purchasing arms, ammunition, military equipment and other munitions; the production of poisonous substances, narcotic drugs and the procedure for their use;

m) the determination of the status and defense of the state border, territorial sea, airspace, exclusive economic zone and continental shelf of the Russian Federation;

n) the organization of courts; the procurator's office; criminal, criminal-procedural and criminal-executive legislation; amnesties and pardons; civil, civil-procedural and arbitration-procedural legislation; the legal regulation of intellectual property;

o) federal conflict of laws;

p) the meteorological service, standards, the metric system and the computation of time; geodesy and cartography; names of geographic features; official statistical and bookkeeping systems and procedures;

q) government awards and honorary titles of the Russian Federation;

r) the federal government civil service.

Article 72

1. The joint authority of the Russian Federation and the members of the Russian Federation shall comprise:

a) ensuring the conformity of the constitutions and laws of republics, the statutes, laws and other normative legal acts of territories, regions, cities of federal importance, the autonomous region, and autonomous areas to the Constitution of the Russian Federation and federal laws;

b) the protection of human and civil rights and freedoms; the protection of the rights of national minorities; the ensuring of law and order and of public security; a regime of border zones;

c) questions related to the possession, use and disposal of lands, minerals, water and other natural resources;

d) the demarcation of state property;

e) nature management; environmental protection and the ensuring of environmental safety; specially protected natural areas; the protection of historic and cultural monuments;

f) general issues of upbringing, education, science, culture, physical culture and sports;

g) coordination of issues of public health; protection of families, mothers, fathers and children; social protection, including social security;

h) the carrying out of measures to cope with catastrophes, natural calamities, epidemics and related clean-up operations;

i) the establishment of general principles for taxation and levies in the Russian Federation;

j) administrative, administrative-procedural, labor, family, housing, land, water and forest legislation; legislation on mineral resources and on environmental protection;

k) personnel of the courts and law enforcement agencies; the legal profession, the office of notary public;

l) the protection of the ancestral habitat and traditional way of life of small ethnic communities;

m) the establishment of general principles for the organization of a system of bodies of state authorities and local self-government;

n) the coordination of the international and external economic relations of the members of the Russian Federation, and the fulfillment of the international treaties of the Russian Federation.

2. The provisions of this article shall apply equally to republics, territories, regions, cities of federal importance, the autonomous region, and autonomous areas.

Article 73

Outside the Russian Federation's scope of authority and the powers of the Russian Federation arising from the joint terms of reference of the Russian Federation and the members of the Russian Federation, the members of the Russian Federation shall enjoy full state power.

Article 74

1. The establishment of customs frontiers, duties, levies or any other barriers to the free movement of goods, services and financial resources shall not be allowed within the Russian Federation.

2. Restrictions on the movement of goods and services may be imposed in accordance with a federal law if it is necessary for ensuring the safety and protection of life and health of people, or to protect nature or culture.

Article 75

1. The monetary unit in the Russian Federation

shall be the ruble. Issuance of money shall be carried out exclusively by the Central Bank of the Russian Federation. The introduction and issue of other money in the Russian Federation shall not be allowed.

2. Protecting and ensuring the stability of the ruble shall be the principal function of the Central Bank of the Russian Federation, which it shall discharge independently from other bodies of state authority.

3. A system of taxes to be collected for the federal budget, and the general principles of taxation and levies in the Russian Federation, shall be established by federal law.

4. State loans shall be issued in the manner specified in federal law and shall be accepted on a voluntary basis

Article 76

1. Within the Russian Federation's terms of reference, federal constitutional laws and federal laws shall be adopted that shall have direct effect throughout the entire territory of the Russian Federation.

2. Within the joint terms of reference of the Russian Federation and the members of the Russian Federation, federal laws and the laws and other normative legal acts of the subjects of the Russian Federation adoptable in conformity with them shall be issued.

3. Federal laws may not contradict federal constitutional laws.

4. Outside the Russian Federation's scope of authority and the joint terms of reference of the Russian Federation and the members of the Russian Federation, republics, territories, regions, cities of federal importance, the autonomous region, and autonomous areas

shall exercise their own legal control, including the adoption of laws and other normative legal acts.

5. The laws and other normative legal acts of the subjects of the Russian Federation may not contradict federal laws adopted in accordance with parts one and two of this Article. In the case of a conflict between a federal law and another act issued in the Russian Federation, the federal law shall prevail.

6. In the case of a conflict between a federal law and a normative legal act of a member of the Russian Federation issued in accordance with Part Four of this Article, the normative legal act of the member of the Russian Federation shall prevail.

Article 77

1. The system of bodies of state authority of republics, territories, regions, cities of federal importance, the autonomous region, and autonomous areas shall be established by the subjects of the Russian Federation independently in accordance with the fundamentals of the constitutional system of the Russian Federation and the general principles of organization of the representative and executive bodies of state authority as specified by a federal law.

2. Within the Russian Federation's jurisdiction and its powers arising from the joint terms of reference of the Russian Federation and the members of the Russian Federation, federal executive bodies and the bodies of executive authority of the members of the Russian Federation shall form a single system of executive authority in the Russian Federation.

Article 78

1. Federal executive bodies for the discharge of

their functions may create their own territorial bodies and appoint the appropriate officials.

2. Federal executive bodies may, by agreement with the bodies of executive authority of members of the Russian Federation, delegate to them the discharge of a part of their functions unless this action is contrary to the Constitution of the Russian Federation or federal laws.

3. The executive bodies of members of the Russian Federation may, by agreement with federal executive bodies, transfer to them the discharge of a part of their functions.

4. The President of the Russian Federation and the Government of the Russian Federation shall ensure, in accordance with the Constitution of the Russian Federation, the discharge of the functions of federal state authority throughout the territory of the Russian Federation.

Article 79

The Russian Federation may participate in interstate associations and delegate to them a part of its functions in accordance with international treaties unless this entails a restriction of human and civil rights and freedoms or is contrary to the fundamentals of the constitutional system of the Russian Federation.

Chapter 4. The President of the Russian Federation

Article 80

1. The President of the Russian Federation shall be the head of state.

2. The President of the Russian Federation shall be

the guarantor of the Constitution of the Russian Federation and human and civil rights and freedoms. In a manner specified in the Constitution of the Russian Federation the President shall take measures to protect the sovereignty, independence and state integrity of the Russian Federation and ensure the coordinated action and interaction of the bodies of state authority.

3. The President of the Russian Federation, in accordance with the Constitution of the Russian Federation and federal laws, shall determine guidelines for the domestic and foreign policy of the state.

4. The President of the Russian Federation, as the head of state, shall represent the Russian Federation domestically and in international relations.

Article 81

1. The President of the Russian Federation shall be elected to office for a term of four years by the citizens of the Russian Federation on the basis of universal, direct and equal suffrage by secret ballot.

2. A citizen of the Russian Federation who has attained the age of thirty-five years and has been resident within the Russian Federation for ten years shall be eligible for the office of President.

3. The same individual shall not be elected to the office of President of the Russian Federation for more than two consecutive terms.

4. The procedure for the election of a President of the Russian Federation shall be determined by federal legislation.

Article 82

1. Before beginning the execution of his office, the

President of the Russian Federation shall take the following oath:

"I do solemnly swear that in executing the office of President of the Russian Federation I will respect and protect human and civil rights and freedoms, observe and defend the Constitution of the Russian Federation, protect the sovereignty, independence, security and integrity of the country, and faithfully serve its people."

2. The oath shall be taken in a solemn ceremony in the presence of the members of the Federation Council, deputies of the State Duma and judges of the Constitutional Court of the Russian Federation.

Article 83

The President of the Russian Federation shall:

a) appoint, with the consent of the State Duma, the Chairman of the Government of the Russian Federation;

b) be entitled to preside over sessions of the Government of the Russian Federation;

c) accept the resignation of the Russian Federation Government;

d) nominate for approval by the State Duma the Chairman of the Central Bank of the Russian Federation and bring before the State Duma the issue of removing the Chairman of the Central Bank of the Russian Federation from office;

e) appoint, based on proposals by the Chairman of the Government of the Russian Federation, Deputy Chairmen of the government of the Russian Federation and federal ministers and remove them from office;

f) nominate judges to the Constitutional Court, Supreme Court and Court of Arbitration of the Russian

Federation and the Prosecutor-General of the Russian Federation for appointment by the Federation Council; submit to the Federation Council a proposal for the dismissal of the Prosecutor-General of the Russian Federation; and appoint judges to other federal courts;

g) organize and chair the Security Council of the Russian Federation, the status of which shall be defined by federal legislation;

h) approve the military doctrine of the Russian Federation;

i) organize the Executive Office (Administration) of the President of the Russian Federation;

j) appoint and dismiss the plenipotentiary representatives of the President of the Russian Federation;

k) appoint and dismiss the top commanders of the Armed Forces of the Russian Federation;

l) appoint and recall, after consultations with the corresponding committees or commissions of the houses of the Federal Assembly, diplomatic representatives of the Russian Federation in foreign countries and international organizations.

Article 84

The President of the Russian Federation shall:

a) call elections to the State Duma in accordance with the Constitution of the Russian Federation and federal legislation;

b) dissolve the State Duma under the circumstances and in accordance with procedures stipulated by the Constitution of the Russian Federation;

c) call a referendum in accordance with procedures stipulated by federal constitutional law;

d) submit bills to the State Duma;

e) sign and make public federal laws;

f) give to the Federal Assembly an annual state of the nation message and a message on guidelines for the domestic and foreign policies of the state.

Article 85

1. The President of the Russian Federation may use reconciliatory procedures in order to settle differences between the bodies of state authority of the Russian Federation and the bodies of state authority of the members of the Russian Federation, as well as between the bodies of state authority of Russian Federation members. If no agreement is achieved, he may send the case to the appropriate court.

2. The President of the Russian Federation shall be entitled to suspend the acts of executive bodies of Russian Federation members if they contradict the Constitution of the Russian Federation, federal laws or the international obligations of the Russian Federation or constitute a breach of human and civil rights and freedoms, until the matter is decided by the appropriate court.

Article 86

The President of the Russian Federation shall:

a) be in charge of the foreign policy of the Russian Federation;

b) conduct negotiations and sign international treaties of the Russian Federation;

c) sign instruments of ratification;

d) accept the credentials and letters of recall of the diplomatic representatives accredited to his office.

Article 87

1. The President of the Russian Federation shall be Commander-in-Chief of the Armed Forces of the Russian Federation.

2. In the case of aggression against the Russian Federation or the direct threat thereof, the President of the Russian Federation shall introduce martial law throughout the territory of the Russian Federation or in some parts thereof and immediately inform the Federation Council and the State Duma of this action.

3. The martial law regime shall be determined by federal constitutional law.

Article 88

The President of the Russian Federation shall, under the circumstances and in accordance with the procedures stipulated by federal constitutional law, announce a state of emergency within the territory of the Russian Federation or some parts thereof and immediately inform the Federation Council and the State Duma of this action.

Article 89

The President of the Russian Federation shall:

a) decide questions of the Russian Federation citizenship and the granting of political asylum;

b) confer state awards of the Russian Federation, honorary titles of the Russian Federation and top military and special titles;

c) grant pardons.

Article 90

1. The President of the Russian Federation shall issue decrees and directives.

2. Decrees and directives of the President of the Russian Federation shall be binding for execution throughout the territory of the Russian Federation.

3. Decrees and directives of the President of the Russian Federation shall not contradict the Constitution of the Russian Federation or federal laws.

Article 91

The President of the Russian Federation shall have immunity.

Article 92

1. The President of the Russian Federation shall commence to execute the office of President with the taking of the oath and shall terminate the execution of the office when his term expires and the next President-elect takes the oath.

2. The President of the Russian Federation shall discontinue the execution of the office before its expiration in cases of resignation, continued inability to discharge the powers and the duties of the office for reasons of health, or removal from office by impeachment. New presidential elections shall be held no later than three months after the early termination of the execution of the office.

3. In case of the inability of the President of the Russian Federation to execute presidential powers and duties, they shall devolve to the Chairman of the Government of the Russian Federation. The acting President of the Russian Federation may not dissolve the State Duma, call a referendum or submit proposals on amendments to the Constitution of the Russian Federation or revisions of its provisions.

Article 93

1. The President of the Russian Federation may only be removed from office by the Federation Council on the grounds of accusations of high treason or of another grave crime advanced by the State Duma, provided the Supreme Court of the Russian Federation qualifies the President's actions as criminal and the Constitutional Court of the Russian Federation concludes that the established procedure for the accusations has been observed.

2. The decision of the State Duma to advance accusations against the President of the Russian Federation and the decision of the Federation Council to remove the President from office shall be passed by two-thirds of the votes of the total number of deputies in each house on the initiative of at least one-third of the State Duma deputies, provided there is a corresponding conclusion by a special commission set up by the State Duma.

3. The decision of the Federation Council to remove the President of the Russian Federation from office shall be adopted no later than three months after the State Duma advances its accusations. If the Federation Council fails to adopt such a decision by this deadline, the accusations against the President of the Russian Federation shall be considered dismissed.

Chapter 5. The Federal Assembly

Article 94

The Federal Assembly – the Parliament of the Russian Federation – shall be the supreme representative and legislative body of the Russian Federation.

Article 95

1. The Federal Assembly shall consist of two houses—a Federation Council and a State Duma.

2. The Federation Council shall be composed of two representatives from each member of the Russian Federation—one from its representative and one from its executive body of state authority.

3. The State Duma shall be composed of 450 deputies.

Article 96

1. The State Duma shall be elected for a term of four years.

2. The procedure for forming the Federation Council and the procedure for electing the deputies of the State Duma shall he determined by federal legislation.

Article 97

1. Any citizen of the Russian Federation who has attained the age of twenty-one years and is qualified to vote may be elected a deputy of the State Duma.

2. No individual shall be a member of the Federation Council and a deputy of the State Duma simultaneously. A deputy of the State Duma shall not be a deputy of any other representative bodies of state authority and/or bodies of local self-government.

3. The deputies of the State Duma shall work on a professional, permanent basis. The deputies of the State Duma may not hold any government office or take other paid jobs, excluding teaching, science and other creative pursuits.

Article 98

1. The members of the Federation Council and

deputies of the State Duma shall be inviolable during the entire term of their office. They may not be taken in custody, arrested and searched, excluding in cases when caught locus delicti, as well as examined, excluding in cases stipulated by federal legislation in order to ensure the security of other individuals.

2. Inviolability shall be lifted by the corresponding house of the Federal Assembly on the recommendation of the Prosecutor-General of the Russian Federation.

Article 99

1. The Federal Assembly shall be a permanently working body.

2. The State Duma shall he convened for its first session on the thirtieth day after its election. The President of the Russian Federation may convene a session of the State Duma at an earlier date.

3. The first session of the State Duma shall be opened by the eldest deputy.

4. The jurisdiction of the previous State Duma shall end the moment the new State Duma begins its work.

Article 100

1. The Federation Council and the State Duma shall have their sessions separately.

2. The sessions of the Federation Council and the State Duma shall be public. In the cases stipulated by their code of procedure, they may hold their sessions in camera.

3. The houses may hold joint sessions to hear the messages of the President of the Russian Federation, the messages of the Constitutional Court of the Russian Federation, and statements by the leaders of foreign states.

Article 101

1. The Federation Council shall elect its Chairman and Deputy Chairmen from among its members. The State Duma shall elect its Chairman and Deputy Chairmen from among its deputies.

2. The Chairman of the Federation Council and his deputies, and the Chairman of the State Duma and his deputies shall preside over the sessions of their respective houses and supervise the observance of their regulations.

3. The Federation Council and the State Duma shall form committees and commissions and hold hearings on the issues within their respective terms of reference.

4. Each of the houses shall adopt its code of procedure and decide matters pertaining to the regulation of its activities.

5. To supervise the execution of the federal budget the Federation Council and the State Duma shall form an Accounting Chamber. Its composition and procedure of work shall be determined by federal legislation.

Article 102

1. The Federation Council shall have power:

    a) to approve changes of borders between members of the Russian Federation;

    b) to approve the decree of the President of the Russian Federation on the introduction of martial law;

    c) to approve the decree of the President of the Russian Federation on the introduction of the state of emergency;

    d) to decide the possibility of using the Armed Forces of the Russian Federation beyond its territory;

e) to call the elections of the President of the Russian Federation;

f) to remove the President of the Russian Federation from office by impeachment;

g) to appoint the judges of the Constitutional Court of the Russian Federation, the Supreme Court of the Russian Federation and the Supreme Court of Arbitration of the Russian Federation;

h) to appoint and remove from office the Prosecutor-General of the Russian Federation;

i) to appoint the Deputy Chairman of the Accounting Chamber and half of its auditors and to remove them from office.

2. The Federation Council shall adopt resolutions on the matters that are within its jurisdiction in accordance with the Constitution of the Russian Federation.

3. The resolutions of the Federation Council shall be adopted by majority vote of the total number of its members, unless a different procedure is stipulated by the Constitution of the Russian Federation.

Article 103

1. The State Duma shall have the power:

a) to approve the nominee of the President of the Russian Federation to the office of the Chairman of the Government of the Russian Federation;

b) to decide questions pertaining to the vote of confidence with regard to the Government of the Russian Federation;

c) to appoint the Chairman of the Central Bank of the Russian Federation and to remove him from office;

d) to appoint the Chairman of the Accounting

Chamber and half of its auditors and to remove them from office;

e) to appoint an Officer for Human Rights, who will act in accordance with a federal constitutional law, and to remove him from office;

f) to declare amnesty;

g) to lodge accusations against the President of the Russian Federation for the purpose of removing him from office by impeachment.

2. The State Duma shall adopt resolutions on the matters that are within its jurisdiction, in accordance with the Constitution of the Russian Federation.

3. The resolutions of the State Duma shall be adopted by majority vote of the total number of its deputies, unless any other procedure is stipulated by the Constitution of the Russian Federation.

Article 104

1. The President of the Russian Federation, the Federation Council, members of the Federation Council, deputies of the State Duma, the Government of the Russian Federation, and the legislative (representative) bodies of the members of the Russian Federation shall have the right to initiate legislation. The Constitutional Court of the Russian Federation, the Supreme Court of the Russian Federation and the Supreme Court of Arbitration of the Russian Federation shall be entitled to initiate legislation on the matters within their respective terms of reference.

2. Bills shall be submitted to the State Duma.

3. Bills on the imposition or elimination of taxes, tax exemption, the issue of state loans and changes in the financial obligations of the state and other bills per-

taining to the expenditures that are covered out of the federal budget may be submitted provided there is a consent of the Government of the Russian Federation.

Article 105

1. The federal laws shall be adopted by the State Duma.

2. The federal laws shall be adopted by majority vote of the total number of deputies to the State Duma, unless a different procedure is stipulated by the Constitution of the Russian Federation.

3. The federal laws adopted by the State Duma shall be submitted for consideration by the Federation Council within a period of five days.

4. A federal law shall be considered adopted by the Federation Council if more than half of the general number of its deputies have voted for it or if it has not been considered by the Federation Council within fourteen days of its submission. If the Federation Council rejects a federal law, the two houses may set up a reconciliatory commission to settle the dispute. After that, the federal law shall be due for repeat consideration by the State Duma.

5. In case of the disagreement of the State Duma with the decision of the Federation Council, a federal law shall be considered adopted if in the repeat voting at least two-thirds of the total number of the State Duma deputies have voted for it.

Article 106

Due for the mandatory consideration by the Federation Council shall be the federal laws adopted by the State Duma on the following matters:

a) the federal budget;

b) federal taxes and levies;

c) financial, currency, credit and customs control and the issue of money;

d) ratification and denunciation of the international treaties of the Russian Federation;

e) the status and protection of the state border of the Russian Federation;

f) war and peace.

Article 107

1. The federal law shall be forwarded to the President of the Russian Federation within five days of its adoption for signing and making public.

2. The President of the Russian Federation shall sign the federal law within fourteen days and make it public.

3. If the President of the Russian Federation rejects a federal law within fourteen days of its submission, the State Duma and Federation Council shall subject it to repeat consideration in accordance with the procedure stipulated by the Constitution of the Russian Federation. If after a repeat consideration the federal law is approved in its previous edition by majority vote of at least two-thirds of the total number of the Federation Council members and State Duma deputies, it should be signed by the President of the Russian Federation within seven days and made public.

Article 108

1. Federal constitutional laws shall be adopted on the matters stipulated by the Constitution of the Russian Federation.

2. The federal constitutional law shall be considered adopted if it has been approved by at least three-

quarters of the total number of the Federation Council members and by at least two-thirds of the total number of State Duma deputies. The adopted federal constitutional law shall be forwarded to the President of the Russian Federation for signing and publicizing within fourteen days of adoption.

Article 109

1. The State Duma may be dissolved by the President of the Russian Federation in the instances provided by Articles 111 and 117 of the Constitution of the Russian Federation.

2. In the event of the dissolution of the State Duma, the President of the Russian Federation shall set the date of elections. The newly elected State Duma should be convened no later than four months after the dissolution.

3. The State Duma may not be dissolved for the reasons laid down in Article 117 of the Constitution of the Russian Federation within the first twelve months of its election.

4. The State Duma may not be dissolved from the moment when it lodges charges against the President of the Russian Federation until the adoption of a corresponding decision by the Federation Council.

5. The State Duma may not be dissolved during a time when martial law or the state of emergency is in effect throughout the entire territory of the Russian Federation, and during a period of six months before the office of the President of the Russian Federation expires.

Chapter 6.
The Government of the Russian Federation

Article 110

1. The executive power of the Russian Federation shall be vested in the Government of the Russian Federation.

2. The government of the Russian Federation shall be composed of the Chairman of the Government of the Russian Federation, Deputy Chairmen of the Government of the Russian Federation and federal ministers.

Article 111

1. The Chairman of the Government of the Russian Federation shall be appointed by the President of the Russian Federation with the consent of the State Duma.

2. The nomination concerning the candidate for the office of Chairman of the Government of the Russian Federation shall be submitted by the newly elected President of the Russian Federation within two weeks of his entering into office or after the resignation of the Government of the Russian Federation, or within a week of the rejection of a candidate by the State Duma.

3. The State Duma shall consider the candidate for the office of Chairman of the Government of the Russian Federation proposed by the President of the Russian Federation within a week of the submission of the nomination of the candidate.

4. After the State Duma rejects three candidates to the office of Chairman of the Government of the Russian Federation, the President of the Russian Federation shall appoint the Chairman of the Government of

the Russian Federation, dissolve the State Duma, and call new elections.

Article 112

1. The Chairman of the Government of the Russian Federation shall submit to the President of the Russian Federation his proposals on the structure of the federal bodies of the executive power not later than one week after his appointment.

2. The Chairman of the Government of the Russian Federation shall propose to the President of the Russian Federation his candidates to the offices of Deputy Chairmen of the Government of the Russian Federation and federal ministers.

Article 113

The Chairman of the Government of the Russian Federation, in accordance with the Constitution of the Russian Federation, federal legislation and decrees of the President of the Russian Federation, shall determine guidelines for the activity of the Government of the Russian Federation and organize its work.

Article 114

1. The Government of the Russian Federation shall have power:

   a) to prepare and submit to the State Duma the federal budget and ensure its execution; submit to the State Duma a report on the implementation of the federal budget;

   b) to ensure the pursuit in the Russian Federation of a uniform financial, credit and monetary policy;

   c) to ensure the pursuit in the Russian Federation of a uniform state policy in the fields of culture,

science, education, health protection, social security
and ecology;

d) to manage federal property;

e) to carry out measures aimed to ensure the defense and state security of the country and the pursuit
of the foreign policy of the Russian Federation;

f) to carry out measures aimed to ensure legality,
protect human rights, personal freedoms and property,
maintain public order and combat crime;

g) to exercise other powers stipulated by the
Constitution of the Russian Federation, federal laws
and decrees of the President of the Russian Federation.

2. Regulations for the activity of the Government of
the Russian Federation shall be determined by a federal
constitutional law.

Article 115

1. On the basis and in pursuit of the Constitution of
the Russian Federation, federal laws and normative
decrees of the President of the Russian Federation, the
government of the Russian Federation shall adopt resolutions and directives and ensure their implementation.

2. The resolutions and directives of the Government
of the Russian Federation shall be binding for execution in the Russian Federation.

3. The resolutions and directives of the Government
of the Russian Federation may be denounced by the
President of the Russian Federation if they contradict
the Constitution of the Russian Federation, federal
laws and decrees of the President of the Russian Federation.

Article 116

The Government of the Russian Federation shall

submit a letter of resignation to the newly elected President of the Russian Federation.

Article 117

1. The government of the Russian Federation shall be entitled to give the offer of resignation, which is either accepted or rejected by the President of the Russian Federation.

2. The President of the Russian Federation may adopt a decision on the resignation of the government of the Russian Federation.

3. The State Duma may give the government of the Russian Federation a vote of no confidence. The resolution on the vote of no confidence to the Government of the Russian Federation shall be adopted by majority vote of the total number of the State Duma deputies. After the State Duma gives the Government of the Russian Federation a vote of no confidence, the President of the Russian Federation may announce the resignation of the government of the Russian Federation or reject the decision of the State Duma. If within the next three months the State Duma again gives the Government a vote of no confidence, the President of the Russian Federation shall announce the resignation of the Government of the Russian Federation or dissolve the State Duma.

4. The Chairman of the Government of the Russian Federation may ask the State Duma to put the question of trust in the government of the Russian Federation to a vote. If the State Duma gives a vote of no confidence, the President, within seven days, shall adopt a decision on the resignation of the Government of the Russian

Federation or the dissolution of the State Duma and the holding of new elections.

5. In the event of the termination of its office or resignation, the government of the Russian Federation, on instructions from the President of the Russian Federation, shall continue to work until a new government of the Russian Federation is formed.

Chapter 7. Judicial Power

Article 118

1. Justice in the Russian Federation shall be administered by the courts of law only.

2. Judicial power shall be effected by means of constitutional, civil, administrative and criminal judicial proceedings.

3. The judicial system of the Russian Federation shall be established by the Constitution of the Russian Federation and federal constitutional law. The creation of emergency courts shall be prohibited

Article 119

Citizens of the Russian Federation who have reached the age of twenty-five, have a higher legal education and have a record of work in the legal profession of no less than five years, may become judges. Federal law may set additional requirements for the judges of the Russian Federation courts.

Article 120

1. Judges shall be independent and subject only to the Constitution of the Russian Federation and federal law.

2. Should a court discover in considering a case that

a decision taken by a state or some other governmental body contravenes a law, it shall accept a decision which is in accordance with the law.

Article 121

1. Judges shall be irremovable.

2. The powers of a judge may be discontinued or suspended only in accordance with the procedure and on the grounds established by federal law.

Article 122

1. Judges shall be inviolable.

2. No judge shall be prosecuted otherwise than in accordance with the procedure established by federal law.

Article 123

1. Proceedings in all courts shall be open. Hearings in camera shall only be allowed in cases provided for by federal law.

2. No criminal charge shall be considered in a court in the absence of the defendant, except for the cases provided for by federal law.

3. Judicial proceedings shall be conducted on the basis of adversary procedure and equality of the parties.

4. Judicial proceedings shall be conducted with the participation of a jury in cases provided for by federal law.

Article 124

Courts shall be financed out of the federal budget only, and in such a way that the courts shall be able to administer justice fully and independently in accordance with federal law.

Article 125

1. The Constitutional Court of the Russian Federation shall be comprised of nineteen judges.

2. At the request of the President of the Russian Federation, the Federation Council, the State Duma, one-fifth of the members of the Federation Council or deputies of the State Duma, the Government of the Russian Federation, the Supreme Court of the Russian Federation, the Supreme Arbitration Court of the Russian Federation and the bodies of legislative and executive power of the members of the Russian Federation, the Constitutional Court of the Russian Federation shall decide cases about the compliance of the following enactments and deeds with the Constitution of the Russian Federation:

a) federal laws and enactments of the President of the Russian Federation, the Federation Council, the State Duma and the Government of the Russian Federation;

b) constitutions of the republics, statutes and also laws and other enactments of the members of the Russian Federation, issued on questions within the jurisdiction of the bodies of state authority of the Russian Federation and joint jurisdiction of the bodies of sate authority of the Russian Federation and bodies of state authority of the members of the Russian Federation;

c) treaties between the bodies of state authority of the Russian Federation and bodies of state authority of the members of the Russian Federation and treaties between the bodies of state authority of the members of the Russian Federation;

d) international treaties of the Russian Federation that have not come into force.

3. The Constitutional Court of the Russian Federation shall settle disputes about competence:

a) between the federal bodies of state authority;

b) between the bodies of state authority of the Russian Federation and bodies of state authority of the members of the Russian Federation;

c) between the highest bodies of state authority of the members of the Russian Federation.

4. In response to complaints about a violation of the constitutional rights and freedoms of citizens and at the request of the courts, the Constitutional Court of the Russian Federation shall verify the constitutionality of a law that has been used or should be used in a specific case, in accordance with the procedure established by federal law.

5. The Constitutional Court of the Russian Federation shall interpret the Constitution of the Russian Federation at the request of the President of the Russian Federation, the Federation Council, the State Duma, the Government of the Russian Federation and the bodies of legislative power of the members of the Russian Federation.

6. Enactments or their individual provisions that have been judged unconstitutional shall be invalid; international treaties of the Russian Federation that contravene the Constitution of the Russian Federation shall not be brought into force and shall not be used.

7. At the request of the Federation Council, the Constitutional Court of the Russian Federation shall

pronounce its judgment about the observance of the established procedure in bringing against the President of the Russian Federation the accusation of high treason or other grave crimes.

Article 126

The Supreme Court of the Russian Federation shall be the highest judicial authority on civil, criminal, administrative and other cases within the jurisdiction of the common pleas courts, shall effect the judicial oversight of their activities in accordance with the procedure established by federal law, and shall give explanations on questions pertaining to legal practice.

Article 127

The Supreme Arbitration Court of the Russian Federation shall be the highest judicial authority in settling economic and other disputes within the jurisdiction of the courts of arbitration, shall oversee the latter's activities in accordance with the procedure established by federal law, and shall give explanations on questions pertaining to legal practice.

Article 128

1. The judges of the Constitutional Court of the Russian Federation, the Supreme Court of the Russian Federation, and the Supreme Arbitration Court of the Russian Federation shall be appointed by the Federation Council upon nomination by the President of the Russian Federation.

2. Judges of the other federal courts shall be appointed by the President of the Russian Federation in accordance with the procedure established by federal law.

3. The powers and the procedure for the creation and activity of the Constitutional Court of the Russian Federation, the Supreme Court of the Russian Federation, the Supreme Arbitration Court of the Russian Federation, and other federal courts, shall be established by federal constitutional law.

Article 129

1. The Prosecutor's Office of the Russian Federation shall constitute a single centralized system, in which the lower-level prosecutors shall be accountable to the higher-level prosecutors and the Prosecutor-General of the Russian Federation.

2. The Prosecutor-General of the Russian Federation shall be appointed and dismissed by the Federation Council on the recommendation of the President of the Russian Federation.

3. The prosecutor of the members of the Russian Federation shall be appointed by the Prosecutor-General of the Russian Federation with the consent of its members.

4. Other prosecutors shall be appointed by the Prosecutor-General of the Russian Federation.

5. The power, organization of work, and the procedure regulating the activities of the Prosecutor's Office of the Russian Federation shall be established by federal law.

Chapter 8. Local Self-Government

Article 130

1. Local self-government within the Russian Federation shall guarantee the population the possibility of

independently solving questions of local importance and owning, using, and managing municipal property.

2. Local self-government shall be effected by citizens through referendums, elections and other means of direct exercise of their will, and through the elected and other bodies of local self-government.

Article 131

1. Local self-government shall be instituted in urban and rural settlements and in other territories with consideration for historical and other local traditions. The structure of the bodies of local self-government shall be determined by the population independently.

2. The borders of territories in which local self-government is instituted may be changed should the population of such territories so desire.

Article 132

1. The bodies of local self-government shall independently manage municipal property; prepare, approve and execute the local budget; establish local taxes and levies; maintain public order; and decide other questions of local importance.

2. The bodies of local self-government may be vested by law with some state powers and shall receive the required material and financial means for the implementation of these powers. The state shall oversee the implementation of these powers.

Article 133

Local self-government within the Russian Federation shall be guaranteed by the right to legal protection, compensation for the additional expenses resulting from the decisions taken by the bodies of state authority, and a ban on restrictions of the rights of local self-government as established by the Constitution of the Russian Federation and other federal laws.

Chapter 9. Constitutional Amendments and Revision of the Constitution

Article 134

Proposals for amending and reviewing any provisions of the Constitution of the Russian Federation may be submitted by the President of the Russian Federation, the Federation Council, the State Duma, the Government of the Russian Federation, the legislative (representative) bodies of the members of the Russian Federation, and a group of at least one-fifth of the members of the Federation Council or deputies of the State Duma.

Article 135

1. No provision contained in Chapters 1, 2 and 9 of the Constitution of the Russian Federation shall be reviewed by the Federal Assembly.

2. Should a proposal for a review of the provision of Chapters 1, 2 and 9 of the Constitution of the Russian Federation receive the support of three-fifths of the total number of members of the Federation Council and deputies of the State Duma, a Constitutional Assembly shall be convened in accordance with the federal constitutional law

3. The Constitutional Assembly shall either confirm the immutability of the Constitution of the Russian Federation or draft a new Constitution of the Russian Federation, which shall be considered passed if it

receives two-thirds of the votes of all members of the Constitutional Assembly, or shall be put to nationwide vote. Should the draft of a new Constitution of the Russian Federation be put to nationwide vote, it shall be considered passed if more than half of the voters who have taken part in the vote have voted for it, provided that more than half of the eligible voters have taken part in the vote.

Article 136

Any amendments to Chapters 3 through 8 of the Constitution of the Russian Federation shall be passed in accordance with the procedure established for the adoption of a federal constitutional law and shall come into force after their approval by the legislative bodies of power of at least two-thirds of the members of the Russian Federation.

Article 137

1. Any change in Article 65 of the Constitution of the Russian Federation, establishing the make-up of the Russian Federation, shall be made on the basis of the federal constitutional law on the Admission to the Russian Federation and creation within it of a new member to the Russian Federation and on the change of the constitutional and legal status of a member of the Russian Federation.

2. Should the name of a republic, territory, region, federal-status city, autonomous region or autonomous area be changed, the new name of the member of the Russian Federation shall be included in Article 65 of the Constitution of the Russian Federation.

PART TWO

Concluding and Transnational Provisions

1. The Constitution of the Russian Federation shall come into force on the day it is officially made public in accordance with the results of the nationwide vote.

December 12, 1993, the day of the nationwide vote, shall be considered the day of the adoption of the Constitution of the Russian Federation.

The Constitution (Fundamental Law) of the Russian Federation – Russia, passed on April 12, 1978, with all its subsequent amendments, shall become null and void simultaneously.

Should the provisions of the Federation Treaty — the Treaty on the Delimitation of Jurisdiction and Powers between the Federal Bodies of State Authority of the Russian Federation and the Bodies of State Authority of the Sovereign Republics within the Russian Federation, the Treaty on the Delimitation of Jurisdiction and Powers between the Federal Bodies of State Authority of the Russian Federation and the Bodies of State Authority of the Territories, Regions and the Cities of Moscow and St. Petersburg, the Treaty on the Delimitation of Jurisdiction and Powers between the Federal Bodies of State Authority of the Russian Federation and the Bodies of State Authority of the Autonomous Region and Autonomous Areas within the Russian Federation and other treaties between the federal bodies of state authority of the Russian Federation and the bodies of state authority of the members of the Russian Federation and treaties between the bodies of state authority of the members of the Russian Federation — contravene those of the Constitution of the Russian Federation, the provisions of the Constitution of the Russian Federation shall apply.

2. All laws and other legal acts enforced throughout the territory of the Russian Federation before this Constitution became effective shall remain valid as long as they do not contravene the Constitution of the Russian Federation.

3. The President of the Russian Federation, elected in accordance with the Constitution (Fundamental Law) of the Russian Federation – Russia, since the day on which this Constitution became effective, shall carry out his duties established by it until the expiration of the term for which he was elected.

4. The Council of Ministers – Government of the Russian Federation, as of the day on which this Constitution shall come into force, shall acquire the rights, duties and responsibility of the Government of the Russian Federation, established by the Constitution of the Russian Federation, and shall be named henceforth the Government of the Russian Federation.

5. The courts in the Russian Federation shall administer justice in accordance with their powers established by this Constitution.

When this Constitution becomes effective, the judges of all courts of the Russian Federation shall retain their powers until the expiration of the term for which they were elected. Vacancies shall be filled in accordance with the procedure established by this Constitution.

6. Until the enforcement of the federal law establishing the procedure for the court hearing of cases with the participation of a jury, the former procedure

for hearing the corresponding cases in court shall be preserved.

Until the law of criminal procedure of the Russian Federation is brought into conformity with the provision of this Constitution, the former procedure for arresting, holding in custody and detaining persons suspected of having committed a crime shall be preserved.

7. The Federation Council of first convocation and the State Duma of first convocation shall be elected for a term of two years.

8. The Federation Council shall meet for its first session on the thirtieth day after its election. The first session of the Federation Council shall be opened by the President of the Russian Federation.

9. A deputy to the State Duma of first convocation may be concurrently a member of the Government of the Russian Federation. The members of the Government of the Russian Federation, who are concurrently deputies to the State Duma, shall not be covered by the provisions of this Constitution concerning the immunity of deputies in the sense of accountability for actions (or inaction) connected with the performance of their official duties.

Deputies to the Federation Council of first convocation shall carry out their duties on a part-time basis.

★ ★ ★

BLOCS, FACTIONS, PARTIES:
THE POLITICAL ANATOMY OF
THE NEW PARLIAMENT OF THE RUSSIAN FEDERA-
TION–THE STATE DUMA
(as of January 1994)

1. **Bloc "Russia's Choice"** (76 seats)
   Leader: Yegor Timurovich Gaidar (born 1956)
   Economist with the doctorate from Moscow State University;
   held numerous ministerial posts under President Yeltsin.
   Dr. Gaidar resigned his ministerial post in January 1994.

2. **Liberal Democratic Party of Russia** (63 seats)
   Leader: Vladimir Volfovich Zhirinovsky (born 1946)
   An attorney; graduate of Moscow State University Law
   School and the Institute of Asian and African Studies.

3. **Agrarian Party** (53 seats)
   Leader: Mikhail Ivanovich Lapshin (born 1934)
   Graduate of the Moscow Institute of International Relations,
   the Moscow Agricultural Academy, and the State Institute
   of Foreign Languages.

4. **The Communist Party of Russia** (45 seats)
   Leader: Gennady Andreyevich Zyuganov (born 1944)
   Graduate of the State Pedagogical Institute of the City of
   Orel, and The Academy of Social Sciences of the Commu-
   nist Party of the Soviet Union.

5. **Party of Russia's Unity and Accord** (30 seats)
   Leader: Sergei Mikhailovich Shakhrai (born 1956)
   Graduate of the Rostov State University Law School with
   specialty in public law and state organization.

6. **Bloc "Yavlinsky-Boldyrev-Lukin"** (25 seats)
   Leader: Grigory Alexeyevich Yavlinsky (born 1952)
   Graduate of the Moscow Institute of National Economy;
   former deputy Prime Minister of the Russian Federation;
   Chairman of the State Commission of Russia on Economic Reforms; Deputy Chairman of the Committee on
   the Effective Guidance of the National Economy; Chairman of an independent Center for Economic and Political
   Research.

7. **"Women of Russia"** (23 seats)
   Leader: Yekaterina Filippovna Lakhova (born 1948)
   University graduate; Chairperson of the Coordinating Committee on Family, Maternity and Childhood Issues under President Yeltsin.

8. **Democratic Party of Russia** (15 seats)
   Leader: Nikolai Iliych Travkin (born 1946)
   Graduate of the Engineering School in the City of Klin and the Pedagogical Institute in the City of Kolomna; former construction worker, engineer, and a functionary of the former Communist Party of the Soviet Union.

9. **Faction "New Regional Policy"** (65 seats)

10. **Independent** (35 seats)

APPENDIX C

SPEAKERS OF THE STATE DUMA AND THE FEDERATION COUNCIL

Speaker of the State Duma:

Ivan Petrovich Rybkin (born 1946)

Graduate of the Agricultural Institute in the City of Volgograd; member of the Agrarian Party and is currently employed with Russia's Ministry of Agriculture. Mr. Rybkin is regarded as a "liberal pro-reform communist."

Speaker of the Federation Council:

Vladimir Filippovich Shumeiko (born 1945)

Graduate of the Polytechnic Institute in the City of Rostov-on-Don. His political and managerial career stretches from a metal worker to a manager of the Krasnoyarsk Measuring Instruments factory; former Deputy Chairmanship of the Supreme Council of the Russian Federation, to Deputy Chairman of the Council of Ministers of the Russian Federation.

APPENDIX D

The Government of the Russian Federation

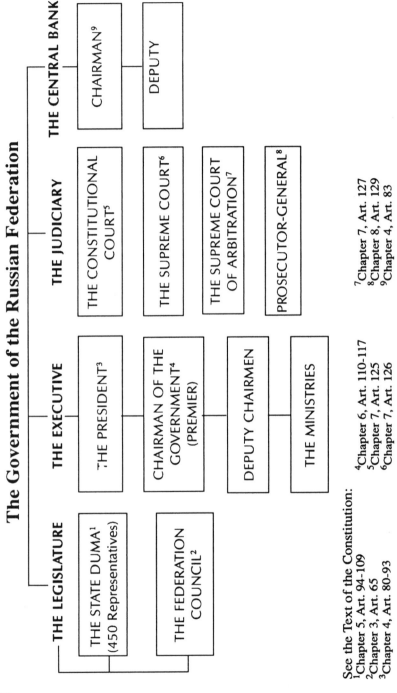

THE LEGISLATURE

THE STATE DUMA[1]
(450 Representatives)

THE FEDERATION COUNCIL[2]

THE EXECUTIVE

THE PRESIDENT[3]

CHAIRMAN OF THE GOVERNMENT[4] (PREMIER)

DEPUTY CHAIRMEN

THE MINISTRIES

THE JUDICIARY

THE CONSTITUTIONAL COURT[5]

THE SUPREME COURT[6]

THE SUPREME COURT OF ARBITRATION[7]

PROSECUTOR-GENERAL[8]

THE CENTRAL BANK

CHAIRMAN[9]

DEPUTY

See the Text of the Constitution:
[1]Chapter 5, Art. 94-109
[2]Chapter 3, Art. 65
[3]Chapter 4, Art. 80-93
[4]Chapter 6, Art. 110-117
[5]Chapter 7, Art. 125
[6]Chapter 7, Art. 126
[7]Chapter 7, Art. 127
[8]Chapter 8, Art. 129
[9]Chapter 4, Art. 83

Leaders of the Soviet Union and The Russian Federation Since the Abdication of the Last Monarch

THE LAST MONARCH
Tsar Nicholas II, 1894-1917, abdicated during the March 1917 Revolution

REPUBLICAN RUSSIA
Prince Georgy Lvov followed by Alexander F. Kerensky, March-November, 1917 (first Premier of the Provisional Government, replaced with the Bolsheviks after the October 1917 Revolution)

DICTATORSHIP OF THE PROLETARIAT
Vladimir I. Lenin (born Vladimir Ilyich Ulyanov; founder of the Communist Party-Bolsheviks; head of state, party, and government), 1917-1924

SOVIET RUSSIA AND THE SOVIET UNION
Collective Leadership by the All Soviet Workers' Party of Bolsheviks
Josef Stalin (born Josef Visarionovich Djugashvili) head of government; Secretary of the Communist Party-Bolsheviks; commander, with the rank of marshal, of all Soviet Armed Forces), 1924-1953

Collegial, Interlocking, Leadership
Georgy M. Malenkov (Premier, head of government); Nikita S. Khrushchov (General Secretary of the CPSU, the ruling party); Klementyi E. Voroshilov (head of state), 1953-1955
Nicolai A. Bulganin (Premier, head of government); Nikita S. Khrushchov (General Secretary of the CPSU, the

ruling party); Klemetyi E. Voroshilov (head of state), 1955-1958 (end of collegial leadership)

Nikita S. Khrushchov (Premier, head of government and General Secretary of the CPSU, the ruling party); Klementyi E. Voroshilov (head of state), 1958-1964

Triple Directorate ("Troyka")

Aleksey N. Kosygin (Premier, head of government); Nikolai V. Podgorny (head of state); Leonid I. Brezhnev (General Secretary of the CPSU and since 1976, the XXV CPSU Congress, head of state—President), 1964-1976

Leonid I. Brezhnev, President and General Secretary of the Communist Party of the Soviet Union, 1976-1982

Yuri V. Andropov, President and General Secretary of the Communist Party of the Soviet Union, 1982-1984

Konstantin U. Chernenko, President and General Secretary of the Communist Party of the Soviet Union

Mikhail S. Gorbachev, President and General Secretary of the Communist Party of the Soviet Union, 1985-1991. Gorbachev resigned resigned on 25 December 1991, and the Soviet Union was dissolved on 26 December 1991.

THE RUSSIAN FEDERATION

Boris Nikolayevich Yeltsin, President of the Russian Federation since 1991. (During the 19 August 1991 coup d'état and the detention and incapacitation of President Gorbachev by the junta, Boris N. Yeltsin served as President of the Russian Federative Republic [elected to that post on 12 June 1991], one of the fifteen republics constituting the Soviet Union.)

APPENDIX F

The Former Soviet Union (USSR)
(Until 25 December 1991, the day its president, Mikhail S. Gorbachev, resigned)

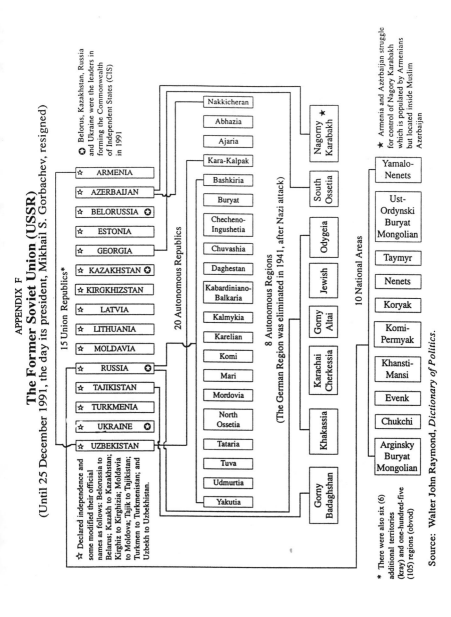

Source: Walter John Raymond, *Dictionary of Politics*.

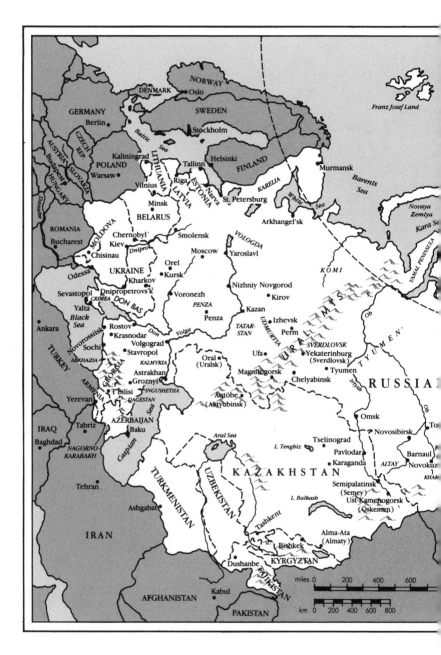

Reprinted by permission from the book *Russia 2010 and What It Means for the World: The CERA Report* by Daniel Yergin and Thane Gustafson. Copyright 1993 by Cambridge Energy Research Associates.

THE FORMER SOVIET UNION

Ocean

ALASKA
(U.S.)

Chukchi
Sea

Bering Strait

St. Lawrence I.
(U.S.)

Wrangel I.

Severnaya
Zemlya

New Siberian Is.

East
Siberian
Sea

Anadyr

Laptev
Sea

Bering Sea

Kolyma

M A G A D A N

Indigirka

VERKHOYANSK MTS.

Lena

Arctic Circle

Y A K U T I A

Magadan

Tunguska

Yakutsk

Lena

Petropavlosk
Kamchatskiy

FEDERATION

Sea of Okhotsk

KAMCHATKA

Aldan

Sakhalin I.

KURILE ISLANDS

Komsomol'sk

L. Baykal

BURYATIA

Khabarovsk

Irkutsk

Chita

Amur

JAPAN

Ulaan Baatar

CHINA

Ussuri

Vladivostok

GOLIA

N. KOREA

Sea of Japan

Beijing

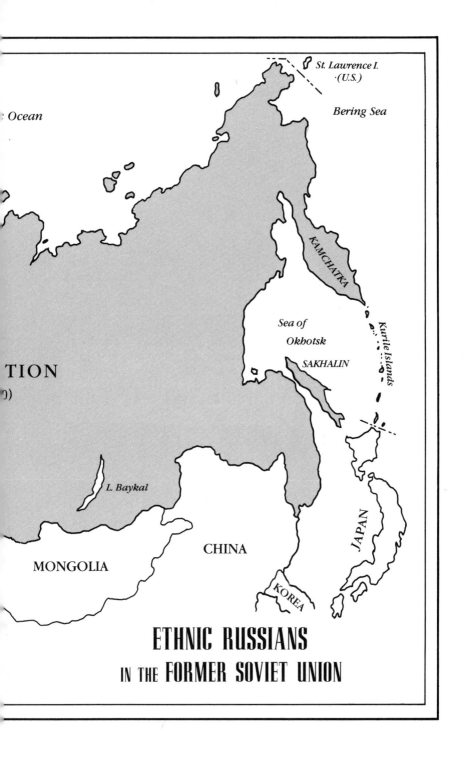

Ocean

St. Lawrence I.
·(U.S.)

Bering Sea

KAMCHATKA

Sea of
Okhotsk

Kurile Islands

SAKHALIN

·TION
·))

L. Baykal

CHINA

JAPAN

MONGOLIA

KOREA

ETHNIC RUSSIANS
IN THE FORMER SOVIET UNION

Available at better bookstores or from the publisher. For prompt delivery, please complete and mail the coupon below.

Please send me:

____*CONSTITUTION OF THE RUSSIAN FEDERATION*
Special Presidential Edition (hardcover) $35.00
plus $5.00 s & h (Virginia residents add $1.35 sales tax)

____*CONSTITUTION OF THE RUSSIAN FEDERATION*
Paperback $12.00
plus $4.00 s & h (Virginia residents add 54 cents sales tax)

____*DICTIONARY OF POLITICS. SELECTED AMERICAN AND
FOREIGN POLITICAL AND LEGAL TERMS.* 7th ed.
by Walter J. Raymond $60.00
plus $5.00 s & h (Virginia residents add $2.70 sales tax)

____*AN ANALYSIS OF JAPANESE PATENT LAW*
translated from the original treatise by Masami Hanabusa $120.00
plus $5.00 s & h (Virginia residents add $5.40 sales tax)

Total $_____

Mail to:

Brunswick Publishing Corporation
ROUTE 1, BOX 1-A-1
LAWRENCEVILLE, VIRGINIA 23868

❏ Check enclosed.   ❏ Charge to my credit card:
❏ VISA   ❏ MasterCard   ❏ American Express

Tel: 804-848-3865 • Fax: 804-848-0607
Charge Card Orders Only — 1-800-336-7154

Card #_____ Exp. Date_____

Signature: _____

Name _____

Address _____

City_____ State_____ Zip _____

Phone # _____